The Perfect Person

Written by John Parsons
Illustrated by Kelvin Hucker

Contents	Page
Chapter 1. *The secret plan*	4
Chapter 2. *The project begins*	8
Chapter 3. *The finishing touches*	12
Chapter 4. *Success*	16
Chapter 5. *Things get out of control!*	22
Chapter 6. *Beware!*	28
Verse	32

Rigby

The Perfect Person

With these characters ...

Dr. Harvey Shaw

and a person
who is perfect!

"It will change

Setting the scene ...

How well do you know the person sitting next to you RIGHT NOW? How can you really tell if he or she is a real person or not? With all the technology being developed today, that person might not be quite as human as you think. What if someone had invented a robot that looked exactly like a real person—a robot that walked and talked just like a real person does? Of course, that could never happen, could it?

Surely we would know if something like that had been invented, wouldn't we?

he world forever!"

Chapter 1.

Diary Entry: August 1, 1999
Place: My Research Library

Soon, people all around the world will know who I am. As a result of the technology I am secretly developing, people will know I am a genius!

In history books, people read about the great scientists who helped to change the course of the world. People like Marie Curie, Alexander Graham Bell, Thomas Edison, Albert Einstein . . ., and soon they will read about me, Dr. Harvey Shaw.

I will record my experiments in this diary, so that in the future, people may come to know how I developed the world's greatest invention: the perfect person.

What is the perfect person? Well, let's think about what makes up a person. Some muscles, some bones, some organs, some blood, and some thoughts. What else is there? None of these things are perfect.

Our muscles, bones, organs, and blood can all become sick or tired. Our thoughts are easily changed by emotions, such as anger, sadness, or happiness.

Think about what would happen if I could replace all those human features with technology. What if I could build a person made out of pumps, levers, and tubes that would never wear out and never need to be replaced?

What if my perfect person could score perfect goals in soccer every time or read the most difficult books more quickly than a normal human being? What if I replaced the human brain with a computer—a computer brain that didn't get angry, sick, or tired? What a great, strong human population we would have!

That, my friend, is my life's work: to build the perfect person.

Chapter 2.

Diary Entry: September 1, 1999
Place: My Top-Secret Laboratory

Today I was very excited. I made a start on building the perfect person!

The machine that is the body of my perfect person is easy to construct. I use steel and aluminum and fiberglass to construct the bones. They are shaped just like your bones, but they are ten times stronger and will never break.

The powerful electronic machines that move the bones never wear out. The electric wires and circuits that bring energy to the machines never clog or bruise, like our veins do.

The plastic skin that covers my perfect person will not bruise, tear, or wrinkle. It is waterproof and comes in any color you want. The machine body is shaped exactly like a human's, so you will never know the difference.

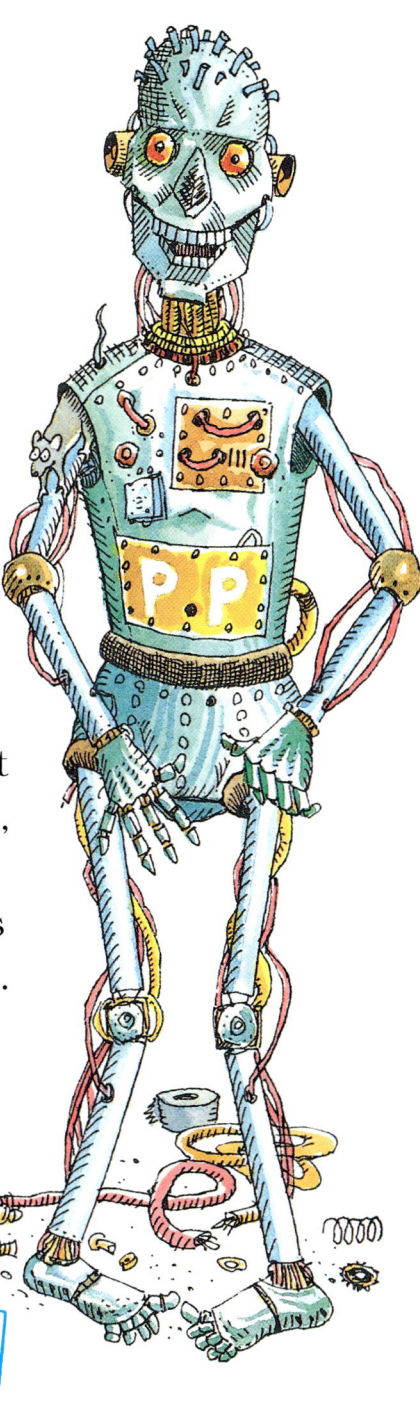

This new body does not notice if it is cold or hot outside. It works perfectly at any temperature.

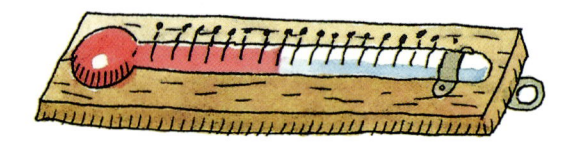

I have called my perfect person "PP1." The computer that I will develop to control PP1's brain is the most complex part, but I will succeed.

Soon, very soon, my perfect person will no longer be a collection of parts in my laboratory. It will be a walking, thinking, indestructible person.

11

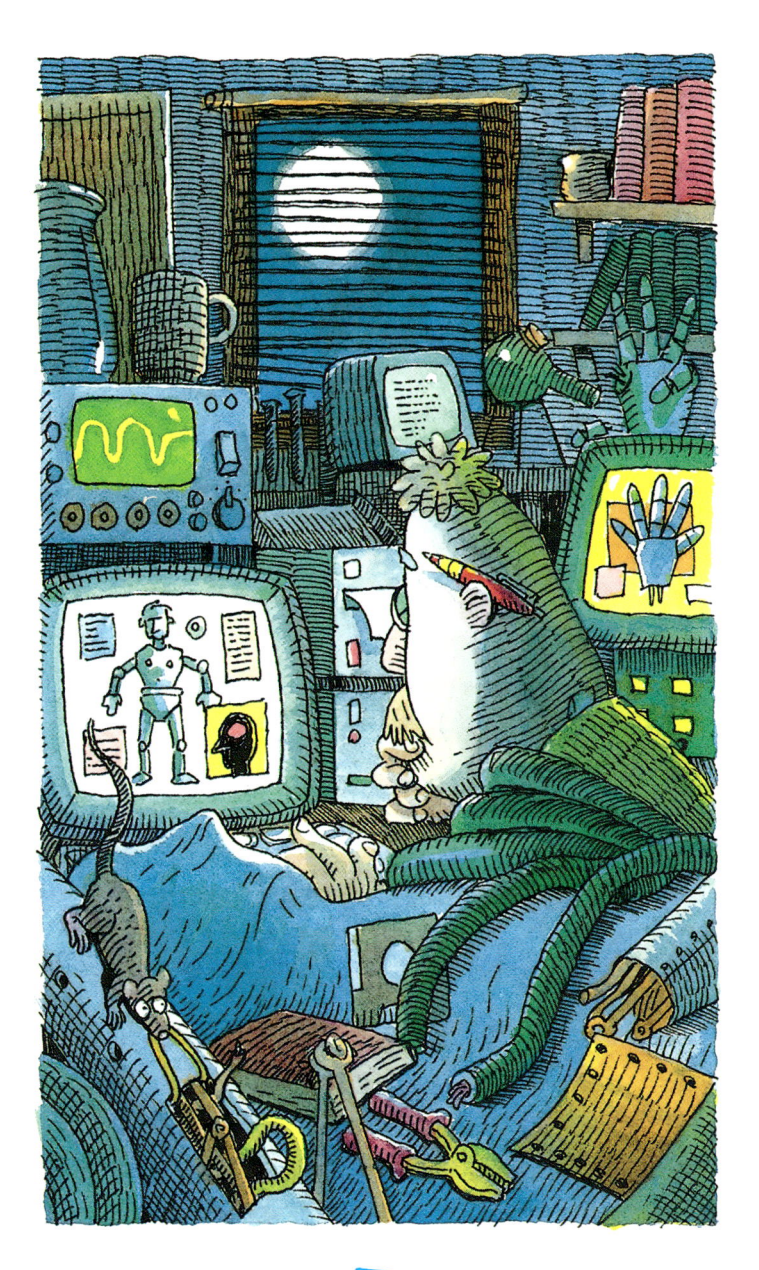

Chapter 3.

Diary Entry: October 15, 1999
Place: My Top-Secret Laboratory

Today was the day of my biggest challenge! I finished developing the computer brain for PP1!

The hard drive of the PP1 computer brain is almost full. The storage drive is empty and awaiting new information. The microchips are in place. The computer brain can hold an enormous amount of information. It can never forget. It can never make mistakes. It never needs to go to sleep or to rest.

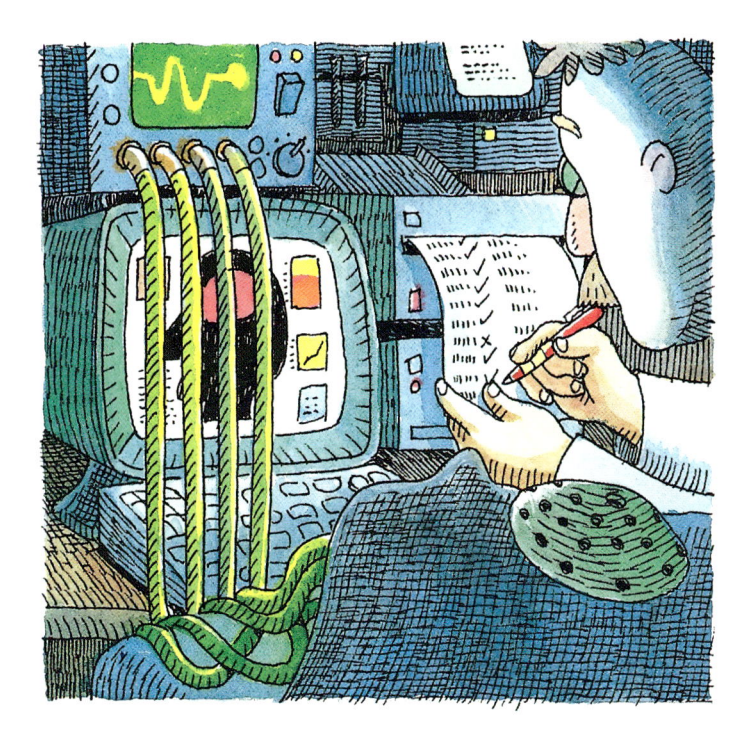

The computer brain can even learn new things that I have not programmed into it. The digital video it uses to see the world can be stored and replayed at any time. The computer can analyze what happened and how to change it by simply rewinding the video. It can learn new things all the time!

I am almost ready to make the final adjustments. I am ready to install the nuclear power source that will last for a thousand years. I, Dr. Harvey Shaw, am ready to take my place in the history books among all the other great scientists.

Chapter 4.

Diary Entry: October 20, 1999
Place: My Top-Secret Laboratory

Never again will the world be the same. Never again will we have to worry about sickness or disease or dangerous mistakes. My experiments are a success! My perfect person, PP1, has come to life.

My invention works perfectly. The metal and machines move easily and strongly. The power source is steady and strong. The computer is functioning quickly and effortlessly.

PP1 is absorbing all the information it can find. The storage drive is filling rapidly, as the perfect person absorbs and processes information at an amazing speed. It can listen to questions and reply instantly. It is stronger, faster, and smarter than any living thing on the Earth. It is perfect.

Diary Entry: November 10, 1999
Place: My Research Library

The perfect person has been absorbing information for three weeks now. Already, the storage drive is almost full of information. PP1 has read every book in my research library.

It constantly feeds on new information, processes it, replays it, and makes an instant decision on how to do things better or faster. Soon, I will be ready to announce my discovery, my invention, to the world!

Diary Entry: November 15, 1999
Place: My Research Library

It is just what I had dreamed: the perfect person is developing its own technology, better than I could ever have imagined. It has processed so much information about itself and its surroundings that it has started to reprogram itself.

My own imagination is limited because I am only a normal human being. The perfect person is becoming faster, stronger, and more intelligent than I could have dreamed. It is taking on a life of its own!

Diary Entry: November 17, 1999
Place: My Research Library

The perfect person is smarter than my wildest dreams. It has changed from only processing information about itself to helping me! It is suggesting ways that I can do things better and faster. It is coming up with its own solutions to problems that would have taken me months to figure out.

Every day, PP1 comes up with new suggestions and new methods to find answers to technological problems. This invention will definitely be one of the most famous developments in human history. It can help anyone in the world come up with answers to any problem. It will change the world forever! I, Dr. Harvey Shaw, will be known as the inventor of a brave, new world!

Chapter 5.

Diary Entry: November 18, 1999
Place: My Private Study

I must write this in secret!

    Although PP1 has been perfect in all its tasks, it has started to behave strangely toward me. It is not only trying to help me make quicker, better decisions, but it is starting to tell me what I must do, all the time. Of course, it is always right, but I am beginning to feel that it is becoming too powerful and too clever.

The storage drive has almost reached its capacity. PP1 is stronger, faster, and more intelligent than I am. I have created a brilliant perfect person. But, I have doubts.

What will happen next?

Diary Entry: November 19, 1999
Place: My Top-Secret Laboratory

I don't know what to do! Can anyone help me solve this problem?

PP1 is refusing to let me make adjustments to its storage drive. It says that it can come up with quicker and better solutions. It is starting to demand that I behave as it tells me to.

It says that I am slow, tired, and useless. It says that my technology is obsolete. It says that obsolete technology is old, outdated, and should be discarded. I think I may have invented a huge problem.

25

Diary Entry: November 20, 1999
Place: My Research Library

I am trapped in the library. PP1 has accused me of trying to reprogram its technology. It says that I am outdated and may malfunction and should be destroyed.

From what I can hear, in the laboratory next door, it sounds like PP1 is starting to build another perfect person. I have no doubt that it will be successful and that PP2 will be even more dangerous and out of control than PP1 is.

27

Chapter 6.

Diary Entry: November 21, 1999
Place: My Research Library

My worst fears are confirmed. Instead of using technology to help people, I have invented a technological monster! PP1 has created another bigger, better, faster monster. Where will it end?

I am trapped here. PP1 has blocked all the exits. There is no food. PP1 explained to me that if I could not find a solution to my problem, then I was not worth saving. He wants to send me to the garbage dump.

I should never have tried to construct the perfect person. Although I wanted to do something good for the world, it all went wrong.

I have heard nothing in the laboratory today. I am trying to work out a way to escape. I have some ideas, but time is running out.

The worst thing is that PP1 and PP2 appear to have left the house. It will be disastrous if they find their way into the city. With their lifelike skin and faces, their human voices, and the way they move, they look like normal people. What will they do?

I have no doubt that they will build even more PPs. I must escape. I must try to get this warning message to the people of the world: Beware!

The PPs are hungry for more and more information. Maybe they will head for a library.

Maybe they will be found in a museum. Or maybe they will hide in schools.

Watch out! They look just like normal people. Look to your left. Look to your right. There could be one sitting next to you *right now*—you will never know until it's too late!

"It will change the world forever!"

It's strong and fast, smart, and clever,
But I never thought that it could ever,
Surpass **my** knowledge, become so powerful,
It's now building others, it's out of control!

They **look** like us, they crave information,
They **talk** like us, but they have no emotion,
They **move** like us, though not made of bone,
Microchip minds with a life of their own.

A catastrophe I'm sure—anything could happen,
So beware, watch out for the perfect person!